A L

# Modern Roses

*Hazel Le Rougetel*

*Illustrated by*

**LIZ PEPPERELL**

*Appletree Press*

First published in 1995 by
The Appletree Press Ltd
19–21 Alfred Street, Belfast BT2 8DL
Tel. +44 (0) 1232 243074
Fax +44 (0) 1232 246756


A Little Book of Modern Roses

A catalogue record for this book is available in The British Library.

ISBN 0-86281-528-2

9 8 7 6 5 4 3 2 1

## ☙ Introduction ❧

In *A Little Book of Old Roses*, 1994, I aimed to follow the development of the rose from early times to the beginning of this century. This new book continues the story until today, tracing the ascendancy of Hybrid Teas and Floribundas with their breeders' emphasis on producing outstanding blooms with good fragrance and, especially important, healthy foliage. At the same time, a great diversity of Modern Shrub Roses was emerging, many with qualities derived from robust species roses: form of growth, distinctive foliage and decorative fruit, as well as flowers.

My interest in Old Roses extended to the development of Hybrid Musks and subsequent shrub roses, but I must confess there has been little time to become conversant with exhibition roses (those grown not only for the show bench, but also for brilliant public display). Therefore I must acknowledge advice from experts in that sphere: Pat Dickson and John Mattock who read and amended the relevant text, and especially the late Jack Harkness for generous guidance as both friend and author.

It was difficult to select twenty-eight roses for illustration from the multitude available today, but a wide spectrum of colour seemed important. However, some one hundred and thirty more are mentioned in the text, the majority of which, with their suppliers, may be traced in *Find That Rose*, an invaluable publication of the British Rose Growers' Association and published yearly. This and the two *Little Books* will help readers to consider growing some older roses with their favourites of today. In writing these books, I have particularly borne in mind owners of small gardens.

## ᏂᏒ 'Peace' ᏥᏅ

'Peace', bred by Francis Meilland of Lyon, must herald any account of Modern Roses, although its story is too well known to repeat in detail here. Its American launch coincided with the fall of Berlin in 1945 and its outstanding qualities of size, colour, strength and health all contributed to the success of this rose, a delicately tinted yellow and pink, making it the most beloved of Hybrid Teas. The first, 'La France' (1867), came from Guillot of Lyon, although the class was not officially recognised until 1879, when Henry Bennett, a Wiltshire farmer, introduced "ten pedigree hybrids of the Tea Rose". His 'Lady Mary Fitzwilliam' (1882) was used by Pernet-Ducher of Lyon to produce 'Madame Caroline Testout' (1890), and by Alexander Dickson of Newtownards, Co. Down for 'Mrs W.J. Grant', the first Hybrid Tea to receive the National Rose Society's Gold Medal in 1892.

Dickson had received fifty-eight gold medals by 1922, a date marking publication of Henslow's *Rose Encyclopaedia*. This book contained some fifty illustrations of elaborate bedding plans from leading nurseries: Dickson showed six large beds of "the best Hybrid Teas" flanking a central pergola which included three of their own breeding – 'K. of K.' (1917), a velvet-sheened solid scarlet, for the middle beds; 'Lady Maureen Stuart' (1920), velvety-black, scarlet-cerise reflexing orangey maroon; and 'Sunstar' (1921), salmon red with deep crimson base. The other two were 'Mrs Henry Morse' (Pernet, 1919) bright rose washed vermilion, introduced by Sam McGredy, the second great Irish breeder, and 'Rev. F. Page Roberts' (1921) golden yellow, from Cant's of Colchester, East Anglia's leading rose establishment.

The earliest Hybrid Teas were of pink or red shades. 'Just Joey', which came from Cant in 1972, is an example of a colour change brought about by Pernet-Ducher in 1900 when, after some years of trial, he introduced 'Soleil d'Or' using bright yellow *Rosa foetida persiana* and a red Hybrid Perpetual as parents. Its many petals were shaded yellow, orange and russet, entirely different from the sober roses bred from 'Parks's Yellow Tea-Scented China'. 'Soleil d'Or' was followed ten years later by 'Rayon d'Or', a true golden-yellow Hybrid Tea, and others which were called Pernetianas until they were merged with Hybrid Teas, bringing new glowing colours to the class.

'Just Joey', a rose of coppery-orange and buff-pink shades, is a Hybrid Tea which has never lost popularity since its introduction, not only for colour, but for cutting and fragrance. Further striking examples of Hybrid Teas bred over the last thirty years include other universal favourites; brilliant vermilion 'Super Star' from Tantau in Germany, orange-pink 'Troika' from Poulsen in Denmark, McGredy's 'Piccadilly', with petals red inside and yellow out, and Dickson's sumptuous 'Tequila Sunrise', bright yellow edged with scarlet.

Although 'Just Joey' makes tremendous impact when massed in beds for public enjoyment, it makes an equal impression when planted informally. At Jenkyn Place, Bentley, near Farnham in Surrey they are planted with bouffant white peonies. Together, they appear perfectly balanced in superb display and, well spaced, each rose showed its loose, fluted petals to advantage, in contrast to the more compact form of its companion.

## ☙ 'Silver Jubilee' ❧

This beautiful Hybrid Tea from Alexander Cocker in Aberdeen was selected to commemorate the twenty-fifth anniversary of the Queen's reign in 1978, appearing on one side of the Jubilee Medal. With its subtle shading of pinks, peach and apricot, it is considered to be among the best in its class and from it, Harkness bred 'Savoy Hotel' (1989), a reliable pink Hybrid Tea.

Of the reds, Albert Norman's 'Ena Harkness', a true crimson, has been acclaimed since its introduction in 1946. Coral-red 'Fragrant Cloud' from Tantau some thirty years later is particularly cherished for its outstanding scent. From this rose, Cocker bred 'Alec's Red', (1970) a deep cherry from darkest maroon buds. Pure white 'Pascali' (1964) won countless awards for Lens of Belgium and an outstanding pale example from Ireland in 1985 gained for Dickson first place in the Rose of the Year Trials, which were held in conjunction with the 1992 Floriade in Holland. It was first known as 'Peaudouce', but now the delicate, softest ivory-lemon Hybrid Tea is called 'Elina'.

An immaculate display of Hybrid Teas and Floribundas can always be found in Queen Mary's Garden, Regent's Park, London, which was commissioned by George V and opened to the public in 1932. The present central rose planting was created by Superintendent Millar Gault in 1955. It has large beds of massed colour surrounded by Climbers and Ramblers which are trained up pillars or swung on swags to create little bowers where visitors may sit to survey the beautiful scene.

Writing in *The Rose Annual* in 1964, Pat Dickson described Floribundas as mixed blooded hybrids, basically from Polyanthas and Hybrid Teas. They have a very long flowering season, a wide variety of clustered forms and are the roses most extensively used in public planting today. The name Floribunda was coined in America and adopted here in 1950 to cover some new introductions as well as a number of large Hybrid Polyanthas which had outgrown the original size of roses in that class.

'Gruss an Aachen' from Geduldig of Germany, 1909, is an example of the latter. It is a splendid rose in every way with an almost continuous supply of large, fully double blooms which echo Old Roses in shape and scent, are coloured cream, peach and pink, and borne on a neat 2 x 2 ft bush. Less compact, 'Nathalie Nypels' was introduced by the Dutch breeder Leenders of Holland in 1919 and is also slightly taller, with a certain grace in its growth and open silvery-pink clustered blooms which are well offset if grown near the silver foliage of *Artemisia canascens*. 'Yvonne Rabier', originally a Polyantha, has small semi-double white flowers in full sprays which are complemented by healthy light green foliage. It came from Turbat of France in 1910, makes a bush of 3 x 2 ft, and seems to flourish in shade.

The great surge of Floribundas did not start until after the Second World War. However, for the small garden, any of the trio above will integrate well in a mixed border with other shrubs and plants, providing flowers over a long period and adding historical interest to a modest collection.

## 'Iceberg'

This Floribunda from Wilhelm Kordes in 1958 was at one time believed to be the most widely grown rose throughout the world. It may be used for bedding, as a standard, or even as a shrub. In fact, it would seem that the glossy light green foliage is healthier without hard pruning and, indeed, the charming buds and pure white blooms are better displayed when grown openly against it. Another white, 'Horstmann's Rosenresli', came from Germany the following year and, although not widely known here, it is eminently suitable for a smaller garden, being of compact bushy growth with well-held abundant clusters of medium-size blooms over three good flushes displayed against faultless foliage.

Among proved pale Floribundas are 'Sea Pearl' (1965) from Dickson, with peach petals reversing to pale yellow, and 'Margaret Merril' (Harkness 1978). The latter is a much-loved rose, not only for its appearance but also for its appealing fragrance. In his *Roses*, 1978, the breeder says that the greatest virtue of this palely blushing rose is scent, often absent from the Floribunda class. Its blooms display gold stamens and grow on strong upright stems.

A fragrant Floribunda from New Zealand, 'Nancy Steen' (Sherwood 1971), was named to honour a cherished New Zealand rosarian; tinted creamy salmon, it is charming – as she was – and is available here. Visiting enthusiasts in the Nelson area of South Island, N.Z., should not miss Tasman Bay Roses, Motueka, where Nigel Pratt displays an attractive and comprehensive collection of old and new roses.

## ꕤ 'Evelyn Fison' ꕤ

A wealth of Floribundas was introduced in the 1960s and 'Evelyn Fison', still in demand, is chosen here as a reliable representative of brilliant reds with healthy foliage. It came from McGredy in 1962, who used it four years later to produce 'City of Belfast', another consistently popular bright red. Cocker's excellent crimson 'Rob Roy' (1970) also had the same parent.

A Californian breeder, Lammerts, named an exceptional Floribunda 'Queen Elizabeth' in 1954 and it is considered to be one of the outstanding roses of this century, universally revered and seemingly tolerant of all conditions. For example, it is grown widely throughout Australia. Its strong upright growth (up to 7 ft) with large clear pink blooms is often used at the back of borders, where it can be fronted by a compact blue-flowered shrub or with shorter roses to hide bare stems, for example, McGredy's 'Elizabeth of Glamis', 1964, or his 'Sexy Rexy', which he bred in New Zealand twenty years later. Both are salmon-pink. Dickson's 'Scented Air' (1965), of the same shade, gained more height through its parent, 'Queen Elizabeth'.

Princess Mary, then Patron of the Royal National Rose Society, opened its new grounds near St. Albans in 1963 and afterwards admired the recently planted roses in the Walk named for her, where 'Iceberg' and 'Allgold' were prominent. Since then the Walk has always been planted with Floribundas and today it is one of the most striking features in the Gardens of the Rose, leading out from the main building and colourful all through the season.

'Allgold', from Edward Le Grice in Norfolk (1956), was one of the best of the early deep yellow Floribundas, and forerunner of many to follow with varying apricot and orange shades. 'Amber Queen' gained Harkness The Rose of the Year Award for 1984 and nine years later had the distinction of being selected for the James Mason Memorial Medal, bestowed on the variety which gave most pleasure over recent years. On that occasion it was well displayed at the British Rose Festival, now held at Hampton Court in July. Aptly named, it has been illustrated here to show its subtle tones, perfectly offset by very dark foliage inherited from 'Southampton' (Harkness 1972) which has darker orange and apricot shades. Harkness also used the latter parent for clear yellow 'Mountbatten' (1982), whose buds were included in Princess Diana's wedding bouquet. This unusually tall Floribunda can be usefully grown as a hedge.

'Korresia' (1977) is another true yellow used for original bedding in Queen Elizabeth The Queen Mother's Rose Walk which leads from her London house in The Mall down to the Lake in St. James's Park. It was presented to her by the National Gardens Scheme on her eightieth birthday. She is the present Patron of the Royal National Rose Society, in whose Gardens the comprehensive display of Old Roses is known as The Queen Mother's Rose Collection. The Award Winners Border is also there and contains those roses successful in the Society's Rose Trials over the last twenty years. It is regularly updated and keeps visitors informed of recently introduced reliable varieties.

Although the answer will be obvious to most people, I am sometimes asked, when lecturing, to describe the difference between Ramblers and Climbers. For any doubtful readers, the explanation is that Ramblers are near hybrids of the invasive, wild species, mostly with small flowers in summer only. Climbers are widely interbred, with larger flowers repeating in autumn.

Climbers of recent date have made little impression, but among many good earlier examples, 'Handel' (McGredy 1965) must be one of the best. Its distinctive colouring of cream petals, edged rose red, intensifies towards the end of the season and its healthy dark foliage makes a good 12 ft display. In the same year, Gregory introduced 'Pink Perpétue', bred from 'Danse de Feu' and 'New Dawn' and this, with its cupped deep pink semi-double flowers, is another good choice of the same height. 'Danse de Feu', from Mallerin in France over forty years ago, has for long been an established favourite. It has 'Paul's Scarlet' (1916) as a parent and its American name, 'Spectacular', describes accurately this striking scarlet rose which is often seen covering walls up to 20 ft.

'Dublin Bay' (McGredy 1976) is shorter, reaching only 7 ft, but will make a good pillar rose with its rich red clusters flowering over a long period. Pillars provide the answer to support shorter roses for those who have no suitable walls for Climbers. Suitably treated wooden posts may be used, but best, I think, are larch branches with side shoots shortened to about 8 inches for a more spectacular open display.

## ღ 'Compassion' ღ

This rose from Harkness in 1973 is recognised as one of the world's best Climbers. Its lovely apricot and pink blooms have a sweet scent, and as the breeder points out, it has an additional asset of freely making basal shoots, an uncommon occurrence in Climbing Hybrid Teas. Through its parents, 'White Cockade' and 'Prima Ballerina' it inherited qualities from both 'New Dawn' and 'Peace'. A sport, 'Highfield' (1982) has paler shades and is slightly shorter than the 10 ft reached by 'Compassion'.

'Meg' (1954), an almost single peachy-pink with dark stamens in a yellow centre, came from Gosset who had used two classic early roses as parents: 'Paul's Lemon Pillar' and the bush form of pale pink 'Madame Butterfly', both dating from the second decade of this century. Most of the Hybrid Tea Climbers are sports from the original bush form, an example being coppery orange 'Mrs. Sam McGredy Climbing', from Holland in 1937, eight years after the original's appearance in Ireland.

'Golden Showers' came from America in 1956. With bright yellow loose petals and distinct glossy foliage, it displays well on pillar or wall and, given enough space, it will make a substantial shrub. 'Alchemist' with its golden-yellow Old Rose full form has a certain charm although it does not repeat in autumn. This rose came from Kordes in 1952 and two years later he introduced 'Leverkusen', another lovely yellow 10 ft Climber, with fluted petals deepening in the centre and offset by glossy light green foliage.

'New Dawn' (1930) occurred as a sport from 'Dr. van Fleet' (1910), a *R. wichuraiana* hybrid named after its American raiser, and its large blooms often class it among Climbers rather than Ramblers. For over six decades it has been a universal favourite, ranking high in popularity lists as an excellent all-purpose rose. It will attain a height of 15 ft given the right situation and can be grown on arch, fence, pergola, pillar, tree or wall, as well as making a splendid standard. In fact, it fulfils Graham Thomas's ideal of a hardy, fragrant, large-flowered rose, climbing gracefully and blooming into late summer. Dark, glistering foliage inherited from *R. wichuraiana*, provides good foil for displaying shapely buds and blushing blooms.

'New Dawn' has been widely used in breeding: Boerner of America produced 'Aloha' (1949) for use as Climber or substantial shrub, with pink petals reversing to deeper pink and with bronze tinted foliage. He also used it with an unnamed yellow Hybrid Tea for 'Coral Dawn' (1952). Cocker crossed it with 'Prima Ballerina' for 'Rosy Mantle' (1968) and with 'Circus' for 'White Cockade' of the following year. These three are all moderate in height and suitable for pillars or walls of a bungalow.

Species and smaller-flowered varieties of clematis, like *C. viticella*, associate well with Climbers. Most flower conveniently either before or after the roses and *C. cirrhosa*, 'The Evergreen Clematis', will adorn a barren rose archway with small white bells from January to March.

Most Ramblers finish flowering by the end of July, but an exception, 'Phyllis Bide', provides the answer for a garden which may only have room for one. It flowers continuously through the season and is a salmon pink and primrose blend with slightly ruffled petals. It came from a Surrey nurseryman, Bide, in 1923. 'Paul Transon' also produces some very fragrant coppery-pink autumn blooms in a good season. Both will reach 10 ft or more, but shorter 'Ghislaine de Féligonde' may also be left to develop into a large bush of soft orange-yellow clustered flowers which bloom over a long period.

A multitude of Ramblers was introduced at the beginning of this century. Among them, 'Blush Rambler' from Cant in 1903 has long been a favourite, as has fragrant 'Sanders' White' (1912) which may be seen at Mottisfont in the National Trust's collection of roses, part of it covering a wall and the rest scrambling effectively at ground level. There, too, deep purplish 'Blue Magenta' combines beautifully with rose-pink 'Débutante' grown over a bower and 'Veilchenblau' maintains soft lilac colours on a shady wall.

Many Ramblers make beautiful weeping standards, one of the best being 'Crimson Shower'. This rose really does pour down large clusters of bright fully double little blooms until September and is admirable for even a tiny garden. 'Kew Rambler' is suitable for growing through a tree. With single pink flowers and greyish foliage inherited from *R. soulieana*, it has a slightly less sophisticated look than others mentioned above.

In his *Climbing Roses Old and New* (1965), Graham Thomas emphasises the beauty of naturally falling sprays of Ramblers growing through trees as opposed to blooms trained upwards by artificial means. To persuade their progress, Gertrude Jekyll used a 14 ft forked pole, as if "painting a picture with an immensely long-handled brush" (*Roses for English Gardens*, 1902). I have *R. helenae* (1907) – discovered in China by E.H. Wilson and named for his wife – growing through a purple prunus where large fragrant white corymbs hang in late July and clusters of small orange-red hips last into winter.

The epic invasive example *R. filipes* 'Kiftsgate', is too rampant for the average garden but three slightly less so are 'Wedding Day' (1950), which arrived as a hybrid in Sir Frederick Stern's Sussex garden, 'Bobbie James' (1960) from Sunningdale Nurseries, Surrey and named after the well-known Yorkshire gardener, and at Sissinghurst Castle in Kent, a Chinese species, *R. mulliganii*, covers a huge frame. All three are white. 'Wedding Day' can be recognised by its ageing, slightly mottled pink flowers. The first two will reach 30 ft, the other only half that height.

*R. davidii*, introduced from China in 1908, is not well known but is certainly well worth considering for situations where tree-climbing giants cannot be accommodated. It reaches only 10 ft and in July bears little clusters of soft pink flowers close to the branches. It is followed by bottle-shaped hips and ornaments my *Acer negundo* 'Variegatum' admirably.

## ঌ 'Cantabrigiensis' ৎ

Among the large bushy species, this is one of the earliest to flower, making a late spring picture with fresh ferny foliage and pale yellow flowers. It was found in the Cambridge Botanic Garden in 1931 and is thought to be a seedling from *R. hugonis* which was collected by Father Hugh Scallon, a missionary, in China, though *R. hugonis* has smaller and darker yellow cupped blooms. A small species of thicket-forming habit, *R. dunwichensis* (a form of East Anglian *R. pimpinellifolia*) is useful to clothe a bank with early cream flowers and later with bronzed foliage.

Of many pink-flowered species, *R. villosa*, once known as 'The Apple Rose', has strong qualities in its large single blooms, downy greyish-green leaves and massive deep orange-crimson hips, while *R. virginiana* is a species to brighten the autumn scene with fiery foliage. Perhaps *R. glauca*, a European species, should be chosen for a garden with room for just one large 6 x 5 ft bush. Its unique foliage, grey-green with tints of mauve and copper, is echoed in the stems and its clear pink, white-centred flowers and mahogany hips provide interest the year through.

*R. soulieana* has fine grey-green foliage, a good foil for its cream flowers and later small orange hips. It is large and lax in growth, but is well displayed at Fairfield House, Hambledon, Hampshire, where the late Peter Wake – one of the best of rose gardeners – devised a splendid method, using inconspicuous stakes and cord, to give support with freedom of growth. This achievement of discreet control presents many species and cultivars to their best advantage in the garden.

## 'Cornelia'

After his involvement with the National Rose Society and exhibition roses for many years, the Reverend Joseph Pemberton moved to Havering-atte-Bower in Essex, where he established a Nursery, turning his attention to breeding autumn-flowering clustered roses. He called them Hybrid Teas until one day, it is said, Courtney Page, the Society's Secretary, observed that their scent was musky and Hybrid Musks they have remained, although it is more likely that fragrance was inherited from *R. multiflora*, through 'Trier' (1904) from Lambert in Germany.

Two of Pemberton's early successes in 1913 were white 'Moonlight' of a robust habit, and neater 'Danäe', which has rich yellow buds opening to cream. Salmon-yellow 'Clytemnestra' (1915) tends to spread. Most Hybrid Musks have healthy, lustrous, often dark foliage, especially cream 'Pax', which has a graceful branching habit. 'Vanity' (1920) has almost single bright pink blooms, effective when planted in a group of three.

Among the best Hybrid Musks are two introduced shortly before Joseph Pemberton died in 1925. 'Penelope' opens to cream from apricot buds. Deadheading this rose after second flowering should be avoided because delightful hips follow, unusually celadon green and coral. Pemberton advocated 'Cornelia' as good for massing and it has all the Hybrid Musk qualities: glossy foliage with coral buds opening to richly scented small salmon-pink rosettes, which are especially colourful in autumn. These roses are ideal for backing borders with tall companions like *Campanula lactiflora* to infill between their flowerings, as can be seen at Newby Hall in Yorkshire.

In 1917, John Bentall, then serving in France, received a letter from his employer, Joseph Pemberton, expressing satisfaction with the substitute gardener – John's wife, Ann. She coped with all tasks, including budding, and when Pemberton became incapacitated in the early 1920s, she took on hybridising as well and no doubt had a hand in producing 'Felicia' (1928), when Pemberton's sister, Florence, managed the Nursery. This is a rewarding Hybrid Musk in form, colour and continuity: the compact 4 x 4 ft bush covered with silvery pink blooms over a long period will grace any garden. I grow it as a floriferous half-standard, well displayed against *Pyrus salicifolia* 'Pendula'.

After the deaths of both Pembertons, the Bentalls set up a Nursery at Brokenbacks in the same Essex village, where Ann continued to breed Hybrid Musks, introducing 'Nancy' with white-eyed red flowers, darker red 'Rosaleen', and deep pink 'Belinda' in the early 1930s. A great triumph came with 'Buff Beauty' (1939). Details of its breeding are unknown, but her son believed one parent was the Noisette 'William Allen Richardson' from which it inherited buff-apricot tones. With more open growth than 'Felicia', the graceful branches will make a bush of 6 x 4 ft, or, if planted against a wall, will rise to twice that height quite happily. An early Bentall catalogue listed 'Sammy' (1921) a carmine, semi-single, thornless rose, suitable for a 4 ft hedge or for bedding. This was one of Ann's favourite Hybrid Musks, now rare, but still grown by Trevor Griffiths, New Zealand's eminent rosarian, seventy years later.

Although she did not breed 'Ballerina' (1937), Ann Bentall had the good sense to evaluate the importance of a chance seedling discovered in the Nursery as her "special little shrub", although her husband did not think much of the small pink white-eyed blooms. Joseph Pemberton had forecast that a time would come when shrub roses would be recognised as a class, but that did not happen until thirty years later when, significantly, both 'Penelope' and 'Ballerina' were highly rated.

Writing in *The Rose Annual*, 1971, Jack Harkness said that a rose he had bred from 'Ballerina" and introduced that year, had given him more pleasure than anything else he had raised. Certainly, it was well named as 'Yesterday', having an echo of Old Roses in its purplish-pink clusters. Three years later he brought out carmine red, white-eyed 'Marjorie Fair', also from 'Ballerina', but slightly shorter. These three roses make most useful moderate-sized shrubs for mid-border. 'Ballerina' has been used in Belgium, where Louis Lens has produced a number of hybrids from it. His list contains 'Poésie' (1985), from 'Ballerina' and 'Moonlight', described as a semi-double white with a pale pink eye and delicate fragrance. Unfortunately, it is not available in Britain.

Had it not been for my chance meeting with Ann's son, her skill as a hybridist would have remained a secret. Jack Bentall carried on at Brokenbacks Nursery and, before his death, had trained his successor, Anastasia Carter, who has collected many early Pemberton and Bentall roses, including 'Havering Rambler' (1915), which has fine foliage and delicate almond pink flowers.

## ꕤ 'The Fairy' ꕤ

This popular little rose, classed as a Dwarf Polyantha, was yet another success for Ann Bentall in 1932. The original bush still blooms in the Nursery. She bred it from an orange Polyantha 'Paul Crampel' and a pink Rambler 'Lady Gay'. One of its advantages is that it starts to flower in late July and carries on through August and September, a lean time for roses. It also has a lax habit and spreading growth (2 x 4 ft), ideal for planting round a small garden pool or for fronting borders, where large clusters of small blooms will tumble gracefully. They are a true rose pink, rare in these days of predominating salmon shades, and will look enchanting with the small blue *Geranium wallichianum* 'Buxton's Variety', another late flowerer.

Small Polyanthas are now being sought by those who want a bright display in a small space over a long period. However, they do tend to sport easily and may produce a surprising assortment of colour. This did not deter the National Trust from planting them in the garden of Blickling Hall in Norfolk. This county has one of the world's most comprehensive collections of old roses at Peter Beales's Attleborough Nursery. Recently, he rediscovered in a garden near the Norfolk Broads a bright crimson Polyantha, 'Miss Edith Cavell' (1917), which originally came from the Dutch breeder, de Ruiter. Scarlet 'Gloria Mundi' and 'Golden Salmon Superieur' in 1929 came from the same source. Today, Gandy's of Lutterworth, Leicestershire, have a good list of Dwarf Polyanthas, including 'Sunshine' (1927) which opens orange and buff from bronze-red buds.

*Rosa rugosa,* from the Far East, is one of the most stalwart of species, its progeny inheriting the ability to thrive in most soil and weather conditions. 'Fru Dagmar Hastrup', a seedling introduced from Germany in 1914, is one of the best. Its compact growth makes an ideal hedge rose, as planted at Castle Howard, and its unusual crimson hips (generally, in *R. rugosa,* they veer towards scarlet) associate well with delicate pink flowers. The exceptional height (up to 8 ft) of 'Sarah van Fleet' (1926) may be used to good effect as a screen of soft lilac-pink semi-double flowers over a long period. Canadians have always specialised in these roses which are tolerant of the harsh climate. Among those in a series named for explorers of the country are double-pink 'Martin Frobisher' (1968) and deeper semi-double 'Jens Munk' (1974), both available in Britain.

*R. rugosa,* when crossed with other species produces sturdy hybrids. 'Max Graf', which resulted from an alliance with *R. wichuraiana* in America, was subsequently used by Kordes for breeding, is low-growing and ideal for covering banks with single pink, white-centred blooms and conspicuous gold stamens. In New Zealand I have seen a striking single crimson hybrid produced by Ken Nobbs, for which he used *R. foliolosa,* an American species, and named 'Ann Endt' for the skilled New Zealand rose gardener. The brilliant autumn foliage and hips of *R. x rugotida* 'Corylus' (1988) in my garden resulted from crossing *R. nitida* with *R. rugosa.*

Some of the Modern Shrub Roses – now officially recognised as the class as Joseph Pemberton had forecast – are described in the next few pages. 'Scarlet Fire' (1952) is one of the most arresting. This rose reaches 10 ft with a most magnificent display of single scarlet-crimson blooms of up to 3 inches in diameter. It flowers over a considerable time and is followed by large bright red hips in autumn and winter. Its breeder, Wilhelm Kordes, emphasises its use in providing shelter for birds. 'Cerise Bouquet' (1958), another of his large spectaculars, has a more spreading habit and a good later crop of brilliant crimson-cerise double flowers borne on arching branches of up to 12 ft in length. The form came from *R. multibracteata* and the flower from 'Crimson Glory', a Hybrid Tea (Kordes, 1935).

In 1927, the Spanish grower, Pedro Dot, introduced an outstanding white rose named 'Nevada' which has always ranked high in any assessment of Shrub Roses. Graham Thomas believes it to be one of the most magnificent. The very large 4 inch single flowers are profusely borne on dark brown stems up to 8 ft in length (Vita Sackville-West called it 'Snowstorm in Summer'). They repeat only intermittently in autumn. Its pink sport, 'Marguerite Hilling' (1959) makes an equally dramatic display. Two chance hybrids of *R. canina*, single pink 'Andersonii' (Hillier 1912) and paler semi-double 'Abbotswood' (Hilling 1954) fruit well on lengthy spreading branches. The latter is spectacular against the distant North Canterbury hills in Sally Allison's extensive collection at 'Lyddington', one of many beautiful private gardens of roses in New Zealand.

## ଓ 'Golden Wings' ଔ

"The unequalled grace of the Wild Rose is as remarkable as the beauty of bloom for which the Rose is grown in gardens" – thus, in 1881 William Robinson had aimed to divert the thoughts of many rose growers then solely interested in exhibiting. His wise counsel has been followed by breeders in this century who appreciate the importance of form, as well as hardiness, in most species. *R. pimpinellifolia grandiflora (altaica)* was used by Roy Shepherd in America to produce 'Golden Wings' (1956), a rose with fragrant clear yellow blooms and conspicuous dark stamens, borne on a branching bush of 5 x 4 ft flowering from June to October.

Kordes also used this parent for his 'Frühling' series, of which once-flowering pale yellow 'Frühlingsgold' (1937) is often seen. 'Frühlingsmorgen' (1941) has some charming later flowers, rose pink and primrose-centred with maroon stamens on a slender 6 ft bush. 'Maigold' (1953) inherited the strain from 'Frühlingstag'. It has semi-double soft gold blooms and grows to 5 x 10 ft. This rose is generally used as an early flowering Climber, but it can also be grown as a sprawling Shrub of up to 12 ft. It tolerates poor soil.

*R. eglanteria* was used by Kordes in breeding 'Gold Busch' (1954). Its blooms are fragrant buff-yellow, semi-double flowers on a broad 5 x 9 ft form and its foliage is sweetbriar-scented. It repeats well. 'Fritz Nobis' (1940), also from Kordes, does not, though it makes a good summer show with semi-double shaded pink flowers covering a 6-ft bush, followed by a good crop of autumn hips.

## 'Erfurt'

Although the majority of Pemberton's Hybrid Musks were not hardy in Germany, that country's great breeder, Wilhelm Kordes, acknowledged that he was fortunate in being able to develop from the cherry-red 'Robin Hood', a race of very hardy continuous-flowering shrub roses. Two of the progeny, carmine-red 'Eva' (1933) and 'Wilhelm' (1934), crimson with purplish shading, proved particularly useful. The first produced 'Erfurt' (1939), a very reliable rose, which always makes a statement in the garden with a fine show of semi-double bright pink cream-centred blooms borne on a 5 x 6 ft bush over a long period. It is grown at Fairfield House. 'Will Scarlet' (1947) appeared as a sport from 'Wilhelm' in Hilling's Surrey nursery and was a new colour in Hybrid Musks, as the name implies. Unlike 'Wilhelm' it has some fragrance, but both produce a good showing of orange-red fruit.

Other roses bred by Kordes from the 'Robin Hood' strain are two from a deep crimson 'Eva' hybrid called 'Hamburg'; orange-scarlet 'Bonn' and double cherry-red 'Elmshorn', both introduced in 1950 and forming rounded bushes. The much taller (up to 8 ft) 'Nymphenburg' (1954) is suitable for a spectacular hedge of almost double flowers with salmon, orange and yellow shades lasting well into autumn.

Ann Bentall told her son that the Reverend Joseph Pemberton was excited when he produced 'Nur Muhul' (1923), his first red Hybrid Musk, its dark carmine fading to soft crimson. He was undoubtedly equally pleased with trials of another red, introduced in 1927, the year after his death, named 'Robin Hood'.

## 'Cardinal Hume'

This rose from Harkness in 1984, with musky scent and somewhat spreading habit (3 x 4 ft), is one of a few modern roses of purplish tones that can be compared with old varieties. When planting both together, two provisos should be borne in mind: the new rose should not be too large in bloom or too brilliant in colour to outclass or clash with the old, thus detracting from their discrete qualities. This is particularly important in a short border where strong orange or scarlet must be avoided; lilac-pink is better than salmon, and soft yellow provides a good contrast. The following four will associate agreeably and infill with autumn colour.

'Rosemary Rose' (1953), from the Dutch breeder de Ruiter, has many-petalled deep rose-pink blooms and almost maroon foliage which contrasts well with the blue-green of Albas. To mark their tercentenary in 1988, Peter Beales introduced 'William and Mary', a Modern Shrub which echoes the shape of roses known in the seventeenth century. It makes a substantial bush of 6 x 4 ft, with crimson-carmine tints enlivening silvery-pink flowers. Two other suitable Hybrid Musks for backing shorter Old Roses are 'Lavender Lassie', from Kordes in 1955, which has the right sort of pink clusters for association with deepest Gallicas and Mosses, and 'Thisbe' (Pemberton, 1918), which is a fragrant semi-double, buff yellow-cream, whose colours can usefully be repeated in companion plants such as species of foxglove and day lily, both adding contrasting shapes of form and foliage.

## ☙ 'Bonica '82' ❧

Another of Meilland's outstanding introductions is illustrated here to represent shrub roses of a more spreading habit than those already described. With a mass of loosely frilled pink flowers blooming over a long period, and with glossy coppery foliage and dimensions of 3 x 6 ft, this rose proved ideal for landscape planting. 'Bonica '82' was the first shrub rose to receive the All America Rose Selection award in 1987.

It now rivals the popularity of 'Iceberg' in Australia, where Ross Roses of Willunga are Meilland agents, and the streets and parkland of nearby Adelaide are admirably ornamented not only with 'Bonica '82', but also with examples from the "Meilland" series of landscape roses: 'White', 'Red', 'Scarlet', 'Alba' and 'Coral'. The late Deane Ross did much to reinstate Heritage Roses as well as being instrumental in creating a Twentieth Century Rose Garden in Adelaide, where all the rose classes described in this *Little Book* are represented and, indeed, come from the period since his grandfather founded the Nursery, now in the hands of the fourth generation. This period garden is a fitting memorial to Deane Ross and his forebears.

'Swany', another low, spreading rose from Meilland, displays clusters of double white flowers against dark foliage inherited from *R. sempervirens*. Slightly less invasive are two roses bred from 'Yesterday' by Ilsink of Holland in 1979: 'Smarty', an almost single pale pink, and 'Red Blanket' which is semi-double and darker.

## ☙ 'Surrey' ❧

John Mattock's great contribution to rose growing has been wide promotion of other people's varieties at his nursery near Oxford, especially those of McGredy in New Zealand, Kordes in Germany and Poulsen in Denmark, three of the most important rose breeders in the world today. They include a red Hybrid Tea, 'Royal William' and a pink Climber 'Summer Wine' from Kordes, also McGredy's orange-red Floribunda 'Trumpeter' and white Miniature ground cover, 'Snow Carpet'.

In the early 1980s three very vigorous ground cover roses from Kordes – 'Grouse', 'Partridge' and 'Pheasant' – inherited both the spreading and lax habit of *R. wichuraiana* and the floriferousness of many free-flowering Floribundas and 'The Fairy'. These were introduced by Mattock into the British rose scene. With a spread of 12–15 ft and a height of about 3–4 ft, they were complemented by the 'Bells' series from Poulsen ('Red', 'White' and 'Pink') of some 4 ft in width, but only half the height.

However, these had only a short flowering season. Before long, low growers with continuous display were introduced by Mattock as the 'County' series. Their average size is 1½ x 3–4 ft and among the most popular are single scarlet 'Suffolk', yellow 'Gwent' and 'Surrey', which was awarded a Gold Medal in 1985. Mattock brought out neat 'Northamptonshire' in 1990, a very attractive soft pink and reminiscent of 'Cécile Brunner' when in flower. Local authorities use Mattock's appropriate County Roses for public planting. As individual plants they fill any garden corner with colour – and scent, in the case of bright yellow 'Norfolk'.

## ♡ 'Sweet Dream' ♡

This is a favourite among Patio Roses, and is sought by many people with limited garden space, where Floribundas may be too large and Miniatures too small. They are, Pat Dickson says, "basically dwarf forms of wichuraiana with certain Miniature blood and, not so often, Floribunda". He has bred many successful varieties including 'Gentle Touch' (Rose of the Year, 1986) which opens pale pink from shapely buds, 'Sweet Magic', a true orange, and vibrant 'Sunseeker', mandarin red, suffused with yellow.

Poulsen's pink 'Little Bo Peep' won the Royal National Rose Society's President's International Trophy for the Best New Rose in 1991. Fryer, another Patio Rose specialist, has produced two successful examples: peach-apricot 'Sweet Dream', which gained Rose of the Year Award in 1988, and 'Top Marks', which repeated this performance four years later – sure indications of the competitive ability of a comparatively new class. 'Top Marks' fills a container of at least 10 in diameter and has small double vermilion flowers which hold their colour over a long period.

As well as being dependable for floriferous display, *R. wichuraiana* foliage, evident in many Patio Roses, is small, dense and glossy. The roses make neat little bushes, suitable for fronting borders in small gardens, such as my own, where this year I planted 'Sweet Dream' with short, palest peach nicotiana in front of 'Gruss an Aachen'and deep lilac *Allium pulchellum* to make a pleasing picture. Both roses flowered almost continuously over many months.

## 'Angela Rippon'

A small pink rose, discovered by a Colonel Roulet in a Swiss village in 1918, was introduced in 1922 by Henri Correvon of Geneva as *Rosa rouletii* and from this all our Miniatures have stemmed. Ralph Moore of California became their outstanding and influential breeder. His bright yellow 'Bit o' Sunshine' (1956) was the first to become widely known and his soft pink 'Stacey Sue' (1976) is still considered best for all round use.

Today, their popularity warrants a place in the Royal National Rose Society Miniature Rose Show where orange-red 'Longleat' and cream, edged with pink, 'Baby Katie' have headed prizewinners. Another successful exhibition variety is rose-red, salmon pink 'Angela Rippon'. It is a good example of a typical Miniature, with blooms less than 2 ins in diameter when fully open, and small leaves and thin stems. These are essentially plants for the garden and there is a comprehensive collection in the Royal National Rose Society Gardens, delightfully displayed on raised beds. Among the best are 'Rugul', a really good yellow, 'Bush Baby', a light salmon pink and 'Baby Masquerade', a red, gold and yellow. 'Cinderella', a white and 'Rosamini', a fuchsia pink, are recommended for greenhouse forcing.

For outdoor use, Miniatures are propagated by budding on a rootstock by nurserymen and should then be treated exactly as larger roses. They should not be confused with those grown from cuttings expressly for the pot trade. Advice on the care and cultivation of pot roses comes from Jim Naylor in *The Rose*, Spring, 1994. He emphasises regular feeding, precise deadheading and under- rather than over-watering. For his guidance on producing a concise assessment of Miniatures here, I am most grateful.

## ☙ 'Heritage' ❧

In his foreword to David Austin's *Old Roses and English Roses* (1992) Graham Thomas sums up this breeder's notable achievement by saying that he has provided roses of grace and beauty for gardens of today. Austin produced English Roses by crossing Old Roses with Hybrid Teas and Floribundas to combine the former's natural grace and fragrance with wide colour range and repeat-flowering habit of the latter. I mention here proved examples of various colours.

The first was 'Constance Spry' (1961), bred from two pinks, Gallica 'Belle Isis' (1845) and Floribunda 'Dainty Bess' (1940). It makes a large 10 ft lax shrub, once-flowering, or may be well displayed as a climber, as seen at Mottisfont, covering a considerable wall area with its bright pink flowers of strong myrrh fragrance. 'Heritage, illustrated here, was introduced in 1984. Its blush-pink, full blooms darkening in the centre, are well held on the bush. This English Rose is cherished by gardeners around the world. 'Mary Rose' (1983), a stronger pink, was named to commemorate the salvage of Henry VIII's warship.

'Gertrude Jekyll' was introduced in 1986. This rose has rosette-shaped flowers of a deep pink and a remarkably strong scent, which is inherited from 'Comte de Chambord' (a rose of the Portland class with Damask ancestry) and an upright vigorous growth. Among the reds, 'L.D. Braithwaite' (1989) is a well-proved rich crimson, flowering freely over a long period and is considered one of the best in the class. 'The Prince', which is slightly shorter, echoes the deep purple shades and scent of some of the old Gallicas.

There seems to be general agreement that this is the best of English Roses. The rich butter-yellow old rose form is phenomenal; the scent, an echo of Victorian Tea Roses, is nostalgic and the name is universally revered. Introduced in 1983 and listed as 4 x 4 ft, it competes well with taller delphiniums at the back of Kiftgate's yellow and blue border. I have also seen it covering a ten-foot archway in the remarkable Rose Garden at Renmark, South Australia, where David Ruston, the continent's outstanding grower and florist, has created a veritable oasis of 3,500 varieties, maintained by irrigation from the Murray River.

Among the pale English Roses, 'English Garden' (1986) has a compact 3 ft form and its soft apricot tones well offset by the glaucous foliage of Jackman's Blue Rue. 'Sharifa Asma' (1989) also makes a neat bush; its blush-pink central petals merge to white edges on slightly cupped flowers which are borne in abundance, while 'Fair Bianca' (1982) is pure white, slim and upright. All three have appealing fragrance and plantings of them have proved most rewarding in the garden of Trotton Old Rectory, near Petersfield, Hampshire.

'Graham Thomas' brings this nutshell history of roses to a conclusion, providing a chance to pay tribute to the celebrated gardener for whom it is named. His painstaking research and meticulous recording as author and artist of neglected Old Roses has restored them to their proper place in any assessment of the *genus*, as exemplified in *The Graham Stuart Thomas Rose Book* (1994).

# Index


Amber Queen 16
Angela Rippon 55

Ballerina 35
Bonica '82 48
Buff Beauty 32

Cantabrigiensis 28
Cardinal Hume 47
Compassion 20
Cornelia 31

Erfurt 44
Evelyn Fison 15

The Fairy 36
Fru Dagmar Hastrup 39

Graham Thomas 59
Golden Wings 43
Gruss an Aachen 11

Handel 19
Heritage 56

Iceberg 12

Just Joey 7

New Dawn 23

Peace 4
Phyllis Bide 24

*Rosa helenae* 27

Scarlet Fire 40
Silver Jubilee 8
Surrey 51
Sweet Dream 52